The Hour

The Hour

A COCKTAIL MANIFESTO

by Bernard DeVoto

ILLUSTRATIONS BY WILLIAM BARSS

Tin House Books

Published by Tin House Books 2010

Reprinted by special arrangement with Houghton Mifflin Harcourt Publishing Company

Published by Tin House Books, Portland, Oregon, and Brooklyn, New York
Distributed to the trade by Publishers Group West, 1700 Fourth St., Berkeley, CA 94710, www.pgw.com

 Library of Congress Cataloging-in-Publication Data
De Voto, Bernard Augustine, 1897-1955.
The hour / Bernard DeVoto ; with illustrations by William Barss.
    p. cm.
Originally published: Boston : Houghton Mifflin, 1951.
ISBN 978-0-9825048-0-2
1. Cocktails. 2. Cocktails--Humor. 3. Drinking customs. I. Title.
TX951.D44 2010
641.8'74—dc22
                        2009038327

First U.S. Edition 2010
Second Printing 2015
Printed in the USA
Interior design by Janet Parker and Diane Chonette
www.tinhouse.com

Contents

Introduction

BY DANIEL HANDLER

FOR A SHORT TIME IN MY CHILDHOOD I THOUGHT MY
father, a certified public accountant, was a bootlegger. Part of this was brought about by an overactive
imagination, fed by too much Carson McCullers
at a tender age, resulting in my confusing of the
terms *moonshining* and *moonlighting*. (Imagine my
anticipation, and then my disappointment, when

1

I heard that Bruce Willis and Cybil Shepard were going to be in a television show about illegal distillation.) But the real reason for my suspicions is that my father, once or twice a year, could be found in the basement fiddling with bottles and funnels. It turned out that he was making "half and half"— that is, sweet and dry vermouth in equal parts, a mixture that my father was no longer able to find commercially and which was a crucial ingredient in the Perfect Manhattan he enjoyed everyday after work. When I asked him why he didn't take an extra second and add both vermouths to each cocktail, rather than puttering at length in dim light over a filthy sink, he gave me a curious look. "To save time," he explained.

A generation later my son had his first martini. He was eighteen months old and it was six o'clock. He had watched me mix my own drink, and indicated with a series of hand gestures and bleats his curiosity to try it. I gave him a sip, and his baby blues watered over. He cried for a few seconds, and then, stretching his arms out, uttered through his tears one of the few words he knew: "More."

This is an absurdly complicated world. We so often want what will only bring us more grief, and our moral and logistical strategies rarely make a whit of sense when we open the basement doors. Since time immemorial, when bitchslapped by this bitter epiphany, we have reached for strong drink—only to find that it is an exemplar of our contradictory ways rather than an antidote for them. Drinking, like existence, is an endless muddle, one of the slipperiest boulders in life's daunting stream—we cling to it for support but end up even wetter than when we started. It destroys individuals and rescues large gatherings. It can tear apart loved ones but bring strangers closer together. It starts fights and ends wars. One drinks a right and proper amount; everyone else drinks either too much or not enough. One's own drinking preferences exhibit refinement and sophistication; everyone else's are suspect, as are everyone else's snobberies, recipes, rules, brands, and styles. Alcohol starts endless debates, and endless debates are best settled over a drink.

Such a state of affairs cries out for clarity, and Bernard DeVoto's splendid book *The Hour* provides it straight up. DeVoto is as clear as gin. There have been other books that have suggested ways to transform the world, along with precise instructions on how to carry out this transformation—the New Testament springs to mind—but few have managed to simultaneously convey the likelihood that any solution to the absurdity of life is likely, also, to be absurd. There are some aspects of *The Hour* that have not aged well—despite DeVoto's decrying, early on, of "male egotism," this book is unlikely to be regarded nowadays as a paragon of gender equality—but the book's unwavering nobility has not dimmed any more than the unwavering nobility of its quest. For us to drink more. Of certain drinks. At six o'clock. But not too much.

Bernard DeVoto's name may not ring a bell now, but people were certainly listening in his time. DeVoto was an historian and a journalist, a scholar and a polemicist, a novelist and a soldier. He curated the papers of Mark Twain and edited the journals of Lewis and Clark. He wrote a column for twenty years at *Harper's Magazine*, incurring the ire of the FBI and the state of Utah. He won the Pulitzer Prize and the National Book Award, and his immense, three-volume history of the American West is still in print and still read, although less in living rooms than in American Studies departments, not so much as history but as a product of its time. DeVoto's work has undergone the common but curious transformation from the canonical to the unfashionable, but if his fame has dimmed, it does not appear to be because he did not do enough but perhaps because he did so much; erudite but distrustful of academia, populist but not pandering, serious but not difficult, his work crosses so many boundaries that nobody knows where to hoist his flag.

In DeVoto's biography, written by none other than Wallace Stegner, *The Hour* is described both as "a piece of humorous cultural patriotism" and "a manual of witchcraft," but that's about all one can find of this little book in the dusty critical studies and largely neglected Web sites dedicated to DeVoto's career. But *The Hour* has been kept alive by a different subculture—that of the cocktail enthusiast. I found the book in the window of a bookstore surrounded by vintage cocktail recipe compendiums—of which I have a modest collection—offering drink concoctions that are fun to read but grotesque to sample, as far too many guests to my home can attest.

DeVoto is likely sputtering in his grave at such company. "There are only two cocktails," *The Hour* proclaims. "The bar manuals and the women's pages of the daily press, I know, print scores of messes to which they give that honorable and glorious name. They are not cocktails, they are slops." He calls instead for either a slug of whiskey—my father's drink, the Manhattan, is "an offense against piety"—or the martini, a mixture of gin and vermouth (the word vodka is not to be found in the book) and nothing else, not even an olive. ("[N]othing can be done with people who put olives in martinis, presumably because in some desolate childhood hour someone refused them a dill pickle and so they go through life lusting for the taste of brine.")

The book continues in this stern, decisive tone, instructing the innocents on everything from alternate ingredients of the martini ("Orange bitters make a good astringent for the face. Never put them in anything that is to be drunk.") to instructions on what to hum while preparing them ("[I]t should be nostalgic but not sentimental, neither barbershop nor jazz, between the choir and the glee club.") But *The Hour* is really after a truth less exacting: that there is a sacredness to the time when the workday ends and the evening begins that ought to be observed with a civilized ritual. Though the book's tone might be described as deadpan fascism, the text offers a freedom of mind and spirit.

Before Tin House made getting *The Hour* much easier, I used to search regularly for copies of this book to give to friends. Once, I called a bookstore some two thousand miles from my home and inquired about their Internet listing.

"Oh yes," the bookseller replied, after she'd gone to check. "We have two copies, actually. Which one do you want?"

"Both of them," I said.

"Actually," she said, "there's only one available. I'm going to buy the other one."

I swear I could hear the glint in her eye. It was the look my father had when he was caught in his elaborate time-saving ritual, and the look my son gave me when he reached for the comfort that made him cry. It was the desire for clarity, in the form of muddle; stability, in the form of intoxication. It is the look I see now in the mirror, with my essay done and the sun setting. It is a desire for *The Hour*. Mix your own.

1

——◦◦◦◦——

The American Spirits

WE ARE A PIOUS PEOPLE BUT A PROUD ONE TOO, AWARE
of a noble lineage and a great inheritance. Let us
candidly admit that there are shameful blemishes
on the American past, of which by far the worst is
rum. Nevertheless we have improved man's lot and
enriched his civilization with rye, bourbon, and the
martini cocktail. In all history has any other nation
done so much? Not by two-thirds.

Whiskey came first; it has been the drink of pa-
triots ever since freedom from her mountain height
unfurled her banner to the air. The American people achieved nationality and Old Monongahely in
a single generation, which should surprise no one
since nations flower swiftly once their genius has
budded. Look, for instance, at the Irish, for many
centuries a breed of half-naked cave dwellers sunk
in ignorance and sin and somewhat given to con-
tentiousness. Then the gentle, learned St. Patrick
appeared among them. He taught them to make
usquebaugh and at once they became the most
cultured people in the world. No one challenged
their supremacy, certainly the Scotch didn't, till in-
spiration crossed the Atlantic and set up a still in
Pennsylvania.

Or look nearer home, at the Indians. Gentler
than the Irish, they were an engaging people whose
trust we repaid with atrocious cruelties. (As when,
after the French had educated them to brandy, we

forced rum on them.) Yet a thoughtful man may wonder whether they had it in them to rise to cultural distinction. They evoke both pity and dismay: north of Mexico they never learned to make a fermented beverage, still less a distilled one. Concede that they had ingenuity and by means of it achieved a marvel: they took a couple of wild grasses and bred them up to corn. But what did they do with corn? Century succeeded century and, regarding it as a mere food, they could not meet the challenge on which, as Mr. Toynbee has pointed out, their hopes of civilization hung. Across the continent, every time the rains came some of the corn stored in their granaries began to rot. Would it be doom, the Age of Polished Stone forever, or toward the stars? The historian watches, his breathing suspended, and sees the pointer settle toward decline. They threw the spoiled stuff out for the birds, angrily reproaching their supernaturals, and never knew that the supernaturals had given them a mash.

13

The Americans got no help from heaven or the saints but they knew what to do with corn. In the heroic age our forefathers invented self-government, the Constitution, and bourbon, and on the way to them they invented rye. ("If I don't get rye whiskey I surely will die" expresses one of Mr. Toynbee's inexorable laws of civilization more succinctly than ever he did.) Our political institutions were shaped by our whiskeys, would be inconceivable without them, and share their nature. They are distilled not only from our native grains but from our native vigor, suavity, generosity, peacefulness, and love of accord. Whoever goes looking for us will find us there.

It is true that the nation has never quite lived up to them. From the beginning a small company have kept idealism alight, but the generality have been content to live less purely and less admirably. The ideal is recognized everywhere; it is embodied in an American folk saying that constitutes our highest

The Americans got
no help from heaven
or the saints
but they knew what
to do with corn.

tribute to a first-class man, "He's a gentleman, a scholar, and a judge of good whiskey." Unhappily it is more often generous than deserved. Anyone who will work hard enough can become a scholar, and nearly anyone can have or acquire gentility, but there are never many judges of good whiskey. Now there are only you and I and a few more. One reason is that there is little good whiskey to judge—we do not hold our fellows to the fullness of the nation's genius.

In the era called Prohibition we lapsed into a barbarism that was all but complete—though that dark time did contribute some graces to our culture. In those days one heard much scorn of Prohibition whiskey, but the truth is that there was just about as much good whiskey then as there had been before or is now. (It was then, moreover, that a taste for Scotch, previously confined to a few rich men who drank an alien liquor as a symbol of conspicuous waste, spread among us—a blight which the true-born American regards as more destructive to the ancient virtues than Communism. Think of it less as a repudiation of our heritage than as the will to believe. If we paid the bootlegger for Scotch, we thought, we might get the Real Old McCoy, though one whiskey is as easily made as another where they print the label and compound the flavoring.) Such good whiskey as existed was hard to find but when hadn't it been? Below the level of the truly good we went on drinking the same stuff we had drunk before. We are still drinking it now. The untutored are, and the unworthy.

The bootlegger, that is, did just what the publican had done during our golden age, when the saloon business was organized on a basis of straightforward, standardized adulteration. Pick up a manual of trade practices published in that vanished time. You will find listed eleven grades of rye or bourbon (up to fifteen in manuals that recognize a more fastidious hierarchy of castes) that the proprietor of an honest place is to compound on his premises. They are arranged in the order of their cost to him. The first five contain no whiskey at all; they are neutral spirits plus water and some sophisticating ingredients; the cheapest one has no flavoring but sugar. Then come five more grades, neutral spirits and whiskey mixed in varying proportions, eight to one in the cheapest, fifty-fifty in the most expensive, plus flavoring and coloring matter. So to the eleventh, which consists of two raw whiskeys in equal amounts, plus a dash of a somewhat better one, plus prune juice to supply body and finesse, and the manual says, "this is considered the finest of all grades, as it contains no spirits." Once you got past the eleventh, you reached unadulterated straight whiskey at its rawest and could then progress by regular steps to the best bonded stock. If you could trust the publican.

Let us contemplate some of the adulterator's art. One of the pests who still intrude on the fellowship

is the knowing man. You have seen him—all too often—take a bottle of whiskey, jiggle it a little (perhaps after graceful ritualistic passes), and then, holding it at a slant, call your attention to the beads that form along the edge, nodding his sagacious head, a connoisseur who can't be fooled. The oldtime saloonkeeper took thought of him. The manual says to take four parts of the oil of sweet almonds (a benzaldehyde from which the prussic acid has been removed), add it to one part of chemically pure sulphuric acid, neutralize the mixture with ammonia, and then dilute the results with twice as much neutral spirits. "This," it remarks, "is used to put an artificial bead on inferior liquors." Or how shall we give our product something like a bourbon taste? Easy enough:

Fusel oil ....64 ounces
Potassium acetate 4   "
Sulphuric acid 4   "
Copper sulphate .... ½   "
Ammonium oxalate .... ½   "
Black oxide of manganese 1   "
Water 8   "

And now, "Place them all in a glass percolator and let them rest for 12 hours. Then percolate and put into a glass still, and distill half a gallon of the Bourbon Oil."

There are formulas for Rye Oil, Cognac Oil, Rum Essence, or whatever else your fancy may run to.

There are compounds that help to make the blend smoother—prune juice (with raisins), peach juice (with apples), "St. John's Bread Extract" (with dates), raisin extract (with licorice), tea extract (with currants). "They are," the instructor says, "harmless and efficient aids both to the liquors and to the pocket." And surely they make for thought.

In our enlightened age we have changed all that, saving the proprietor so much hand labor. We have shifted the burden of adulteration from him to a working partnership between the manufacturer and the Bureau of Internal Revenue. We have, however, retained the frankness of the manuals. Everything—or at least quite a bit—is printed on the label for you to see. If you want less fusel oil, which is removed by the distilling process but restored in the flavoring extract, you can climb through the hierarchy at your pleasure. If you trust the bar. Do not be cynical: there are some bars which you can trust and which will serve you no more adulterants than you may order by brand name. But of these how many can you trust not to practice dilution? If you have found one—and you will from time to time—you have found a precious thing and you are a judge of good whiskey.

Never be cynical about bars, in fact, though it is right to be wary. A glory of American culture is that

there is no place so far and no village so small that you cannot find a bar when you want to. (True, in some of the ruder states it must present itself fictitiously as a club or nostalgically as a speakeasy.) Many are more resourceful than the label admits, many others water their whiskey, many are bad or even lousy. Almost all provide instruction for an inquiring mind in the cubic capacity of glassware and how the eye may be misled by the shape and the hand by weight. But do not scorn any of them, not even the neon-lighted or the television-equipped, for any may sustain you in a needful hour. And each of us knows a fair number of good bars and perhaps even a great one. The good bar extends across America, the quiet place, the place that answers to your mood, the upholder of the tavern's great tradition, the welcoming shelter and refuge and sanctuary—and any man of virtue and studious habits may count on finding it. If you hear of any I've missed, let me know. Let us all know.

But a bar, though often a necessity and often
an ornament of culture, is for a need, a whim, or
perhaps an urgency. For the fleeting hour. For the
moment—the high moment, or the low. For, perhaps, the meeting—and may her eyes warm and
sparkle when she comes in the door, ten minutes
late so that you will always be one up on her. You
could not meet her at a better place. Long ago, on
52nd Street I—but let that go. I was saying, bars
are a convenience, an assist, a stay and an uphold-
ing, but the Americans are a home-loving people
and the best place for the devotions proper to
their autochthonous liquors is the home. And let's
be fair: though there is never much good whiskey,
there is always enough to take care of those who
can appreciate it. The surest proof of the moral
foundation of the universe is that you can always
find good whiskey if you will go looking for it.
Resolution, obstinacy, and the spirit of our pio-
neers will take you to it in the end, though you had

better provide yourself with thick-soled shoes for the route may be hard and is certain to be long— and beset with gyps, liars, and the knowing man. I don't know why but there are more brands of good rye than there are of bourbon. And I don't know why the God-damned Navy is permitted to monopolize so many of them—but there's a tip for you. Keep green your friendships in the service, for at any time the officers' store may have an excellent one that a commisary (one who has not crystallized his tonsils to rock-candy with rum) found on a back road in West Virginia and bought up. I have struck Navy installations a thousand miles from salt water and five hundred miles from fresh that had ryes worth traveling fully that far for—yes, worth listening to commanders talk about MacArthur.

But don't let me get garrulous so early in the evening. I was saying, there are a lot of sound four-year-old and eight-year-old ryes that seldom or

The surest proof of the
moral foundation
of the universe is that
you can always find
good whiskey if you will
go looking for it.

———◦◦◦———

never get advertised. Maybe there are more small distilleries that make rye—the family stillhouse in the vale—and maybe that counts. Or maybe it's that I'm a rye man myself. But there they are. A wholesaler who has grace and enlightenment buys them, or a club does, or you have intuitive friends or a sudden streak of luck. Regional ryes, perhaps, but by no means small ones. . . . You have your obligations. If you find one new to you, the rest of us are to hear about it. And the dealer's name.

Well, you say, how good is good whiskey? Out in the bourbon country where the honor of the taste buds runs 180-proof, you can get an argument in ten seconds and a duel in five minutes by asserting that it is as good as it used to be. Here the little stillhouse comes in again. Men grown reverend and wise will tell you that the glory departed when the big combine bought up the family distillery. They are remembering their youth and the smell of mash in a hundred Kentucky valleys. There was art then, they say, and the good red liquor had the integrity of the artist and his soul too, and between Old Benevolence and Old Mr. This there were differences of individuality but none of pride, and how shall America have heroes again, or even men, with this dead-level nonentity they force us to drink now?

They scandalize and horrify the modern distiller. The little stillhouse, he tells you, was steadily poisoning Kentucky. The old-time distiller's mash was not only uncontrolled and vagrant—he got his feet in it and no doubt his hogs too, and it spoiled on him or went contrary or deceived him. Those remembered subtleties were only impurities, or maybe eccentricities of the still going haywire, or the leniency of the gauger, or most likely an old man's lies. He himself with his prime grains, his pedigreed yeast, his scientific procedures controlled to the sixth decimal place, and his automatic machinery that protects everything from the clumsiness and corruption of human hands—he is making better bourbon than the melancholy gaffers ever tasted in the old time.

We have run into a mass of legend and folklore. It reveals that we are a studious people and serious about serious things, but it does make for prejudice and vulgar error. (You want to know where I stand? You must never besmirch yourself with a blend, son—what do you suppose bond is for?) Devoted men, hewing their way through it, have come out with one finding that leans a little toward the opinion of the elders. The old-time distillers, known locally as the priesthood, put their whiskey into bond at less than proof, that is with the percentage of alcohol below fifty. Four years of the aging process brought it up to proof and they bottled it as it was, uncut. The modern distiller, known everywhere as a servant of the people, impelled by government regulation and the higher excise, bonds his stuff at a few per cent above proof. Aging in bond increases

31

the percentage still more, so after bottling he cuts it back to proof with water.

There is instruction here: when you add water to whiskey, you change the taste. In the moment of pure devotion, therefore, the faithful drink it straight. . . . See to it that your demeanor is decorous and seemly at that moment. Attentively but slowly, with the poise of a confidence that has never been betrayed since the Founding Fathers, with due consciousness that providence has bestowed a surpassing bounty on the Americans or that they have earned it for themselves. Our more self-conscious brethren, the oenophilists, are good men too and must not be dispraised, but they vaingloriously claim more than we can allow. Their vintages do indeed have many beauties and blessings and subtleties but they are not superior to ours, only different. True rye and true bourbon wake delight like any great wine with a rich and magical plenitude of overtones and rhymes and resolved dissonances

and a contrapuntal succession of fleeting after-
tastes. They dignify man as possessing a palate that
responds to them and ennoble his soul as shimmer-
ing with the response.

The modern distiller will tell you that whiskey
comes to full maturity in its sixth year, that thereafter its quality falls off. The truth is not in him, do
not give him heed, and why for a hundred and sev-
enty years have sound distillers, and quacks too,
used the adjective "Old" in their brand names? He
obviously does not believe himself. At mounting
expense he keeps some of his product in bond for
eight years and charges correspondingly, and the
result is well worth the mark-up. Eight years is the
longest period for which he can get bond but at still
greater expense he keeps some in the wood for four
years more—and with a twelve-year-old whiskey to
point to, Americans can hold their peace and let
who will praise alien civilizations. The distiller will
also tell you that nothing happens to the finest after

Our more self-conscious
brethren, the oenophilists,
are good men too
and must not be dispraised,
but they vaingloriously claim
more than we can allow.

it is bottled, and again he is wrong. He is especially wrong about rye. In the spacious time when taxes increased the cost of whiskey by only five hundred per cent (it is several thousand now) the wise and provident and kindly bought it by the keg, in fact bought kegs up to their ability to pay, and bottled it themselves in due time and laid it away for their posterity. Better to inherit a rye so laid away in 1915 than great riches. I have known women past their youth and of no blatant charm to make happy marriages because Uncle John, deplored by the family all his life long as a wastrel, had made them his residuary legatee. There is no better warranty of success in marriage; an helpmeet so dowered will hold her husband's loyalty and tenderness secure. A rye thus kept becomes an evanescence, essential grace. It is not to be drunk but only tasted and to be tasted only when one is conscious of having lived purely.

And in a world growing daily more bleak with science, it is good to know that art keeps its secrecies.

Just as the scientists have never learned precisely what happens in the emulsion of a photographic film when light strikes it, so their most exhaustive researches have never let them in on what happens to whiskey during the aging process. There is paradox: the alcohol should leave it before the water does but the alcohol remains and some of the water goes, no one knows why or whither. There is mystery: what happens does so not in the wood of the keg or in the char that has been burned on its surface but in the zone between them, which is quite imaginary but somehow there. And what happens is beyond analysis by chemistry or anything else—simply, a tendency that whiskey shares with man and all his works, a tendency to live by its baser self, departs from it and the good triumphs. Who wants to know? Enough that whiskey becomes, sometimes, good whiskey. (Here the fellowship will shout: Glory!)

For the palate's sake, then, we drink whiskey straight. We drink it straight too in patriotic com-

memoration of the dead who made us a great nation. They walked up to the bar, stood on their
own two feet or on one foot if the rail had been
polished that morning, and called for whiskey
straight in confident expectation and awareness of
the national destiny, and we were a sound society,
and without fear.

All those decades, all those bars. The Holland
House or the Astor House or the St. Nicholas
toward which the Englishman on tour made by
hackney coach from the boat, so that the mag-
nificence of the New World could burst on him
in his first hour—such acres of mirrors, such
mountains of glasses, such gas chandeliers tipped
with a thousand points of flame, and all the ryes
and bourbons of a continent to cleanse away the
peat-taste of his Scotch. The Knickerbocker . . . I
had at least this break from fate, that I got here
in time to know the Knickerbocker. It has been
exactly reproduced in the most beautiful corner

of paradise, with the starry heavens stretching away, admission by card only and saints to serve a probationary period before they can get cards. The Murray Hill, the Parker House, the Planters House, the St. Francis—the Silver Dollar, Joe's Place, the Last Chance Saloon—river boats and tents at the railhead and tables set up under the elms when the clergy met in convocation or the young gentlemen graduated from college—the last Americans in knee breeches, the first in trousers, deacons in black broadcloth, planters in white linen, cordwainers and longshoremen and principals of seminaries for young women and hard-rock men and conductors on the steam cars and circuit riders and editors and rivermen and sportsmen and peddlers—twenty-two hundred counties, forty-eight states, the outlying possessions. The roads ran out in dust or windswept grass and we went on, we came to a river no one had crossed and we forded it, the land angled upward and we climbed to the ridge and exulted, the desert stretched ahead and we plunged into it—and always the honeybee flew ahead of us and there was a hooker of the real stuff at day's end and one for the road tomorrow. Nothing stopped us from sea to shining sea, nothing could stop us, the jug was plugged tight with a corncob, and we built new commonwealths and constitutions and distilleries as we traveled, the world gaped, and destiny said here's how.

But there are times when neither the palate nor patriotism is to be consulted and this is a versatile distillate, ministering to many needs. That other supreme American gift to world culture, the martini, will do only at its own hour. But man's lot is hard and distressful and he may want a drink at almost any hour—midafternoon, after dinner, at midnight, and some say in the morning. (These last drink rum—to hell with them.) At such times you may add water to the American spirits. Charged water is permitted with rye, if you like it that way, and in the splendid city of St. Louis, where civilization took residence long before the Yankees stopped honing their crabbedness on rum, call it "seltzer." But always plain water with the corn-spirit and the good will of a united people shows in the localisms, "bourbon and branch water" our brethren say south of Mason's and Dixon's Line, "bourbon and ditch" west of the hundredth meridian. (You may detect the presence of the Adversary by a faint odor of brimstone and a request for ginger ale.) And, except when you are in a wayward mood, no ice. Ice is for cocktails.

The water bids our genius show its gentleness, taking you by the hand and leading you as softly as the flowers breathe toward loving-kindness. Or as the homing bird soars on unmoving wings at eventide. On this firm foundation the Republic stands. In England they call for a division and the ministry falls, in Russia they shoot a thousand commissars, but in freedom's land they recess, speak the

That other
supreme American
gift to world culture,
the martini,
will do only
at its own hour.

hallowed names of Daniel Webster and Henry Clay, and send out for a statesman's standby and some soda. Strife ceases, the middle way is found, the bill gets passed, and none shall break our union.

But, first of all, this touch softer than woman's is to restore you and me to humanity. I do not need the record, a priest, or a philosopher to remind me what I am—timorous, blundering, self-deceived, preposterous, ground down by failure and betrayal of the dream, evidence that though mankind has developed past the earthworm it has not got much farther. And you, you don't fool me, I know you all too well, I need only look at you or hear you speak. If you were to quote the catechism, "God made me," you would be lying and on the edge of blasphemy, or over the edge.

The hell we are. This is merely a moroseness of tired and buffeted men, an illusion, and help is at hand to brush it away. When weariness and discouragement come upon us there are many things we

might put into our heads to steal away our brains —
Marx, the *Koran* of abstainers, *Mein Kampf*, address-
es made at Commencement or on Mother's Day, the
Chicago Tribune. But we were nourished in a tradition of goodness and the right and we don't, and I'll
have mine with soda but not drowned. The barb is
blunted, the knife sheathed; a star appears above the
treetop, the harsh voices of fools die out, and all un-
seen there was a fire burning on the hearth. In a few
minutes we will see each other as we truly are, sound
men, stout hearts, lovers of the true and upholders
of the good. There's a good deal in what you're saying
and you say it marvelously well. Dismay, annoyance,
resentment—we should have remembered that they
are traps the world sets for the unwary. The battle is
to the brave, the game to the skillful, the day's job to
who shall do it fortified. We needed only a moment
of quickening, a reminder by wisdom laced with a
little water that there are dignity and gallant deeds
and dauntlessness and disregard of the odds, that

44

evil yields and the shadows flee away. A moment of renewal and then get back in there and pitch, we're doing all right. Well, maybe a short one—and hey, there's Bill, get him over here for a minute, a man needs to be told it's all a lie.

The alchemists never found the philosopher's stone but they knew that when they did it would, by a process in which distillation succeeded fermentation, transmute base metals into gold. They were on the right track, they made a good start, and American genius finished the job. I give you: Confusion to the enemies of the Republic.

2

For the Wayward and Beguiled

THE FELLOWSHIP AVOIDS CONTROVERSY BUT MUST
sometimes accept it nevertheless or even precipitate
it. Though a small company, we need fear no threat
brought against us from without but error or dissen-
sion within our ranks could bring us down. That is
why in austere dedication to American culture I now
venture into a field where no one can say anything

without being violently attacked—and attacked by virtuous men who err only through ignorance, not sin. One of our greatest arts is in danger. The worst is, this threat comes from schismatics and heretics within our small band of true believers who should be of one united heart to hold our frontiers against the heathen. Error stalks the streets and disputation has brought darkness over the land. I am not one to withhold the light. I know how many enraged fanatics will jam the offices of Western Union as soon as they catch sight of my text. But I know too that sometimes wisdom has its victories. To recall to wisdom some who have strayed from it and to discover wisdom to some who have sought but not found it, I proceed to explain the philosophy of the martini cocktail.

First we must understand what, functionally, a cocktail is. I will inquire into no man's reasons for taking a drink at any hour except 6:00 p.m. They are his affair and he has a rich variety of liquors to choose from according to his whim or need; may they reward him according to his deserts and well beyond. But when evening quickens in the street, comes a pause in the day's occupation that is known as the cocktail hour. It marks the lifeward turn. The heart wakens from coma and its dyspnea ends. Its strengthening pulse is to cross over into campground, to believe that the world has not been altogether lost or, if lost, then not altogether in vain. But it cannot make the grade alone. It needs help; it needs, my brethren, all the help it can get. It needs a wife (or some other charming woman) of attuned impulse and equal impatience and maybe two or three friends, but no more than two or three. These gathered together in a softly lighted room and, with them what it needs most of all, the bounty of alcohol. Hence the cocktail. After dinner you may, if you like, spend an hour or so sipping a jigger of whiskey diluted to any attenuation that matches your whim with soda or branch water.

But at 6:00 P.M. we must have action. When we summon life to reveal forgotten benisons and give us ourselves again, we do so peremptorily. Confirm that hope, set the beacon burning, and be quick about it. So no water.

There are only two cocktails. The bar manuals and the women's pages of the daily press, I know, print scores of messes to which they give that honorable and glorious name. They are not cocktails, they are slops. They are fit to be drunk only in the barbarian marches and mostly are drunk there, by the barbarians. It is, however, a fact of great sadness that, as well, sometimes they are drunk by people of good will, people fit for our fellowship. We will labor to bring them out of the darkness they wander in, charitably assuming that they wander there as victims of history. I have shown that our forefathers were a great people: they invented rye and bourbon. They were also a tough people: nothing so clearly proves it as that they survived

50

the fearful mixtures they also invented and then drank. A defect of their qualities, I suspect, led them into abomination. They had the restless mind, the instinct to experiment and make combinations. We got radar from that instinct, and Congress, and the Hearst press, and many other marvelous or mysterious works. And we got, four generations ago, in a sudden blight, mixtures of all the known ferments and distillates that whim, malice, mathematics, or an evil imagination could devise. When the instinct reached an apex of genius, we must remember, it flowered into the martini. But it bequeathed us too a sore heritage of the slops I have mentioned, and as the twentieth century came on the most ominous of these was probably the Bronx.

For the Bronx was fashionable. The gay dogs of the Murray Hill Age drank it, the boulevardiers who wore boaters with a string to the left lapel and winked at Gibson Girls as far up Fifth Avenue as

**Whiskey and
vermouth cannot meet
as friends and the
Manhattan is an offense
against piety.**

59th Street. It had the kind of cachet that Maxim's had, or Delmonico's, or say the splendid Richard Harding Davis at the more splendid Knickerbocker bar, or O. Henry in his cellar restaurant, or the bearded (or Van Dyke-ed) critics of Park Row. The Bronx had orange juice in it. It spawned the still more regrettable Orange Blossom. Infection spread and there were worse compounds on the same base, as I shall shudderingly have to say at some length later on. And then, swiftly, came the Plague and the rush of the barbarians in its wake, and all the juices of the orchard went into cocktails. Now, bathtub gin was not a good liquor—though, gentlemen, there have been worse and still are. But it was not bathtub gin that came close to destroying the American stomach, nervous system, and aspiration toward a subtler life. Not the gin but the fruit juices so basely mixed with it: all pestilential, all gangrenous, and all vile. A cocktail does not contain fruit juice.

In that sudden roar the word you make out is "Daiquiri." Yes, yes, I know. I have alluded to rum before, we must not deny that it exists and is drunk, and as a historian I must give it its due. It gave us political freedom and Negro slavery. It got ships built and sailed, forests felled, iron smelted, and commercial freight carried from place to place by men who, if their primordial capitalist bosses had not given them rum, would have done something to get their wages raised. In both cheapness and effectiveness it proved the best liquor for Indian traders to debauch their customers with. People without taste buds can enjoy it now, though the head that follows it is enormous, and such sentimentalists as the seadogs of small sailing craft can believe they do. But mainly it is drunk as all sweet liquors are, in a regressive fantasy, a sad hope of regaining childhood's joy at the soda fountain. No believer could drink it straight or gentled at the fastidious and hopeful hour. No one should drink it with a corrosive added, which is the formula of the Daiquiri.

There are only two cocktails. One can be described straightforwardly. It is a slug of whiskey and it is an honest drink. Those who hold by it at 6:00 P.M. offend no canon of our fellowship. Scotch Irish, rye, bourbon at your will—but of itself alone. Whiskey and vermouth cannot meet as friends and the Manhattan is an offense against piety. With dry vermouth it is disreputable, with sweet vermouth disgusting. It signifies that the drinker, if male, has no spiritual dignity and would really prefer white mule; if female, a banana split.

To make a slug of whiskey, you pour some whiskey on some ice. (Lately the fashionables have been saying "whiskey on the rocks"; suffer them patiently. But do not let tolerance get out of hand. A few months ago in Chicago, at a once respectable bar, I was offered "Whiskey on the Blarney Stone"—the ice was colored green. Let the place be interdicted

and its proprietor put to the torture.) The slug of
whiskey is functional; its lines are clean. Perhaps
the friend for whom you make it will want two or
three drops of bitters. Fine: there is no harm in
bitters, so long as they are Angostura—all others
are condiments for a tea-shoppe cookbook. If he
wants fruit salad in it, remind him that cocktails
are drunk, not eaten, but go along with him as far
as a thin halfslice of orange or, better, one of lemon
peel. Deny him pineapple, cherries, and such truck
as you would cyanide. If he asks for sugar, tell him
you put it in to begin with, and thereafter be wary
in your dealings with him. For sugar means that
he is backsliding and will soon cross the frontier
to join the heathen, with bottles of grenadine and
almond extract in his pack. But before you give a
slug of whiskey to anyone be sure that it is cold.
Cocktails are cold.

  With the other cocktail we reach a fine and noble art, and we reach too the wars over the gospel

that have parted brothers, wrecked marriages, and made enemies of friends. It is here that the heresies burgeon and the schismatics bay. I suppose it is natural enough. Those who seek the perfect thing must have intense natures; there are many roads for them to take, all difficult, none lighted more than fitfully. No wonder if they mistake marsh fires for light, or when they find a light believe it is the only one. From their love comes their tirelessness to defend and praise their love—tenaciously, arrogantly, intolerantly, vindictively. We may understand how cults form with the martini as with all arts, how rituals develop, how superstitious or even sorcerous beliefs and practices betray a faith that is passionate and pure but runs easily to fanaticism. But though we understand these matters we must not be lenient toward them for they divide the fellowship. Always remember that differences among ourselves will give arms to the heathen. Frighten a woman with a bit of ritual and you may produce a hostess who will serve Manhattans. Affront a man with cultish snobbery and you may turn him, God forbid, to rum.

For instance there is a widespread notion that women cannot make martinis, just as some islanders believe that they cast an evil spell on the tribal fishnets. This is a vagrant item of male egotism: the art of the martini is not a sex-linked character. Of men and women alike it requires only intelligence and care—oh, perhaps some additional inborn spiritual fineness, some feeling for artistic form which, if it isn't genius, will do quite as well. Or take the superstition, for I cannot dignify it as a heresy, that the martini must not be shaken. Nonsense. This perfect thing is made of gin and vermouth. They are self-reliant liquors, stable, of stout heart; we do not have to treat them as if they were plover's eggs. It does not matter in the least whether you shake a martini or stir it. It does matter if splinters of ice get into the cocktail glass, and I suppose this small seed of

fact is what grew into the absurdity that we must not "bruise the gin." The gin will take all you are capable of giving it, and so will the vermouth. An old hand will probably use a simple glass pitcher, as convenient or functional; it has no top and so cannot readily be shaken. But if a friend has given you a shaker, there are bar strainers in the world and you need have no ice splinters in your martinis. (The strainer made of spiral wire conduces to language that is unseemly at the cocktail hour; get one that has perforations instead.)

A martini, I repeat, is made of gin and vermouth. Dry vermouth. Besides many bad vermouths, French, Italian, and domestic, there are many good ones. With a devoted spirit keep looking for one that will go harmoniously with the gin of your choice and is dependably uniform in taste. You have found a friend; stay with it. Stay with them both, store them in quantity lest mischance or sudden want overtake you, and in a world of change you will be able to count on your martinis from season unto season, year to year.

Heresies more vicious than these vindicate the instinct of the faithful to do their drinking in their homes. We have proved our friends but anyone else's invitation to a cocktail party or casual suggestion that we stop by for a drink may take us to a house where martinis are made of sweet vermouth or of sweet mixed with dry. It is a grievous betrayal of trust; the bottles should not even be kept on neighboring shelves, still less brought near the martini pitcher. Indeed, sweet vermouth should not be kept on any shelf in my house or yours; the heathen put it to many uses but we know none for it. And, I suppose, nothing can be done with people who put olives in martinis, presumably because in some desolate childhood hour someone refused them a dill pickle and so they go through life lusting for the taste of brine. Something can be done with people who put pickled onions in:

strangulation seems best.* But there is a deadlier
enemy than these, the man who mixes his martinis
beforehand and keeps them in the refrigerator till
cocktail time. You can no more keep a martini in
the refrigerator than you can keep a kiss there. The
proper union of gin and vermouth is a great and
sudden glory; it is one of the happiest marriages on
earth and one of the shortest-lived. The fragile tie
of ecstasy is broken in a few minutes, and thereafter there can be no remarriage. The beforehander

---

* One tribe of our enemies drink something they call a Gibson.
They are not drinking a cocktail, they are drinking gin with an onion in it. Still, it is well to know the name. The cocktail hour may
overtake you sometime when you are far from any bar you know.
It is never safe to order a martini at a strange bar—order a slug of
whiskey. But if you feel venturesome, you may get some leading by
waiting till someone else is served a martini. If it has a pronounced
color the bartender is a felon, and you will be farther along toward
your desire if you order a Gibson and command him to leave the
onion out.

This is the violet hour,
the hour of hush and wonder,
when the affections glow
and valor is reborn...

———⟨ஐ⟩———

has not understood that what is left, though it was once a martini, can never be one again. He has sinned as seriously as the man who leaves some in the pitcher to drown.

A voice from the floor reminds me that there may be dire emergencies. True, though not in your own home; they usually come when some hostess whose favorite drink is green mint mixed with whipping cream asks you to make martinis. She has sweet vermouth—she is the one who buys it. Well, make the proportion practically unthinkable, say seven to one—and remind your companions that the product has a high muzzle velocity. If she has sherry you will be much better off. Govern the proportions according to its dryness; five to one will do if it is very dry, and put a pinch of common table salt into the pitcher. These drinks are not martinis, they are only understudies, but they damn no souls. They are incomparably better than Manhattans, marshmallows, or rum.

Sound practice begins with ice. There must be a lot of it, much more than the catechumen dreams, so much that the gin smokes when you pour it in. A friend of mine has said it for all time; his formula ends "and five hundred pounds of ice." Fill the pitcher with ice, whirl it till dew forms on the glass, pour out the melt, put in another handful of ice. Then as swiftly as possible pour in the gin and vermouth, at once bring the mixture as close to the freezing point of alcohol as can be reached outside the laboratory, and pour out the martinis. You must be unhurried but you must work fast, for a diluted martini would be a contradiction in terms, a violation of nature's order. That is why the art requires so much ice and why the artist will never mix more than a single round at a time, counting noses.

And I'm sorry, you are not a bartender. There are cultists whose pride is to achieve the right proportion by instinct, innate talent, the color of the mixture, or what Aunt Fanny said about born cooks.

They are the extreme fanatics and would almost as soon drink an Alexander as measure out their wares. I honor a great many of them who have served me sound martinis made with what they thought of as perfected skill. I honor them—but the martinis vary from round to round, and one or another must fall short of perfected skill. Serenely accept the cultist's scorn and measure your quantities with an extra glass.

There is a point at which the marriage of gin and vermouth is consummated. It varies a little with the constituents, but for a gin of 94.4 proof and a harmonious vermouth it may be generalized at about 3.7 to one. And that is not only the proper proportion but the critical one; if you use less gin it is a marriage in name only and the name is not martini. You get a drinkable and even pleasurable result, but not art's sunburst of imagined delight becoming real. Happily, the upper limit is not so fixed; you may make it four to one or a little more than that, which is a comfort if you cannot do fractions in your head and an assurance when you must use an unfamiliar gin. But not much more. This is the violet hour, the hour of hush and wonder, when the affections glow and valor is reborn, when the shadows deepen along the edge of the forest and we believe that, if we watch carefully, at any moment we may see the unicorn. But it would not be a martini if we should see him.

So made, the martini is only one brush stroke short of the perfect thing, and I will rebuke no one who likes to leave it there. But the final brush stroke is a few drops of oil squeezed from lemon rind on the surface of each cocktail. Some drop the squeezed bit into the glass; I do not favor the practice and caution you to make it rind, not peel, if you do. And, of course, you will use cocktail glasses, not cups of silver or any other metal, and they will have stems so that heat will not pass from your hand to the martini. Purists chill them before the first round. If any of that round (or any other) is left in the pitcher, throw it away.

The goal is purification and that will begin after the first round has been poured, so I see no need for preliminary spiritual exercises. But it is best approached with a tranquil mind, lest the necessary speed become haste. Tranquility ought normally to come with sight of the familiar bottles. If it doesn't, feel free to hum some simple tune as you go about your preparations; it should be nostalgic but not sentimental, neither barbershop nor jazz, between the choir and the glee club. Do not whistle, for your companions are sinking into the quiet of expectation. And you need not sing, for presently there will be singing in your heart.

3

The Enemy

WE CAN'T SIT AROUND ALL AFTERNOON; THERE IS EVIL to be dealt with. We might as well begin with the soda fountain, for that is where a lot of it begins and I have already shown you the distressing spectacle of people trying to get back there by way of cointreau and white mint or rum and Coca-Cola. Americans are too indulgent to their children; they give them too much money to spend on sweets. I

71

don't suppose the stuff does them any immediate harm but it does give them false values. Chocolate, maple syrup, two dozen other syrups; marshmallow, fudge, butterscotch, two dozen other goos; the whole catalogue of pops, tonics, phosphates, and trademarked soft drinks that would corrode any plumbing except a growing child's — they may seem innocent but they aren't. An ice cream soda can set a child's feet in the path that ends in grenadine, and when you see someone drinking drambuie, créme de menthe, Old Tom gin, or all three stirred together and topped with a maraschino cherry, you must remember that he got that way from pineapple milkshakes long ago. Pity him if you like but treat him as you would a carrier of typhoid. For if the Republic ever comes crashing down, the ruin will have been wrought by this lust for sweet drinks.

Then there are publishers. They are usually regarded as servants of the good life and it's true that many of them, as individuals, do live soundly, with impeccable observances, with marked devotion to good liquor. But that only shows that we can never relax our vigilance anywhere, in any circumstance of life. For there is no publisher in the United States who has not spread infection far more widely than all the typhoid carriers who ever lived. That they have succeeded in getting the virus into your home and mine doesn't matter for we are immune to it. But they have got it there. Go out to the kitchen and look at the books your wife keeps on the shelf. Pick up one and glance through it. Then think of the American homes that have not been immunized.

I'm talking about cookbooks. Every publishing house has from three to a dozen of them and they are money in the bank. Soon or late, usually not very late, this season's novel about the bitch with the compassionate heart in rural Georgia or the court of Louis XV stops selling. A cookbook never does. In season or out, fat years or lean, it is the mainstay

And, I suppose, nothing can
be done with people
who put olives in martinis,
presumably because in some
desolate childhood hour
someone refused them a
dill pickle...

of the publishing business. The grandchildren of
the author, who lived in the era when recipes began
"take four pounds of butter and four dozen eggs,"
set up trust funds for their grandchildren, and the
publisher loves them more warmly than the novelist who makes Book-of-the-Month Club every
time. I don't know how many cookbooks are sold
but it must be upwards of a million copies a year.
Every copy has enough virus in it to infect a city of
fifty thousand; every copy is a recruiting office for
the enemy.

Presumably when the plates are worn out and
a new edition is called for the publisher hires
someone to go over and check the recipes in all
sections but one. If he finds some solecism about
chervil, out it comes. I dare say, even, that they
sometimes actually make and taste the white sauce
to see whether someone has pulled a howler. But
the section fraudulently labeled "Beverages" has
stood unmodified since it was first perpetrated; no

one has bothered to so much as correct the typo-
graphical errors. Furthermore, it is the same in all
cookbooks, having gone out of copyright in 1895.
And if the time when it was written was the lush
days of four pounds of butter in the pantry, it was
also the holy-horror era in our drinking mores. As
I have shown, the basic idea was to see how many
ingredients you could put into a drink, especially a
cocktail, and still survive. Year by year, that mania
of our national adolescence killed more Americans
than smallpox, the Colt revolver, or the Indians.
Yet publishers go on indorsing the same toxins to
more than a million women a year.

For it's women who buy cookbooks and women
who use the Beverage section. Their male counterparts own comically written ptomaine-manuals
stolen from Jerry Thomas and bound in stainproof
covers, called *Jolly Drinking*; *Prosit, Folks*; or *The
Gent's Guide to Bartending*. (These too are com-
missioned, printed, and sold by publishers.) I am

not concerned with the married women who use them—usually married to the counterparts—unless you think it possible to sterilize or massacre them on a sufficiently rewarding scale. But I am concerned about some women for they could be saved.

No doubt the publishers would plead *caveat emptor,* it's no skin off their nose, anyone who has to go to a cookbook to find out how a cocktail is made deserves anything she may find there. Demurrer disallowed: we are entitled to protection, if she isn't. We already know about the married wench and it's our own fault if we ever give her a second chance to come up to us with an arch smile, holding out a glass of liquid distemper and saying "Bet you can't guess what's in this." But these books come into the hands of women who aren't married. Some of them may be attractive, all are at least well-meaning, and a moment of unwariness or even simple good manners may land any of us at a party

that one of them has worked up from a cookbook. The courts of Massachusetts do not hesitate to suppress, in the name of public safety, a book that concedes the existence of two sexes or the possession by one of them of a bifurcated bosom. Is there no threat to the public safety in a book which directs a good-looking girl to serve the identical formula that turned Great-Uncle Harry's kidneys to pumice and brought him to the grave thirty years before his time?

This subject is as repugnant to me as it can possibly be to you but we have got to face what goes on. Passing over twenty pages of emetics and mickey finns compounded on other bases which the cookbook assures a hostess are wonderful, take a look at what can be, and is, done with gin. In the first two of five pages devoted to what it calls "gin cocktails" I find formulas, each under a jolly name, that tell a woman to add to honest gin: grenadine; chartreuse; crème de menthe; grenadine, lemon juice, and egg white; cherry brandy, kirsch, sweet cider, and raspberry syrup; cointreau and lemon juice; crème de menthe, egg white, lemon juice, and orange juice; lime juice and apricot brandy; claret, orange juice, and Jamaica ginger; grenadine, egg white, lemon juice, orange bitters, and sugar—and, so help me God, a seizure that says to mix gin two to one with port and add a dash of orange bitters. Merely to read the formulas paralyzes the stomach muscles for as much as twenty minutes and a single sip would send the iron dog of the epoch they originated in galloping toward the nearest fire hydrant. But there you are. These books are sold freely over the counter, even in these days of national peril. A perfectly nice woman might obey any of those instructions—and don't forget for a moment that she might offer the result to you.

She is probably about twenty-seven, give or take a couple of years, and let's do what we can for her. She has lived alone too long, she had a happy childhood, and nobody has ever told her that childhood's sweet tooth is how she went wrong. (By the way, never accept a divorced woman's invitation to cocktails until you have looked into her divorce; it may very well have resulted from something that began "take a cupful of gin and four tablespoonfuls of grenadine.") She is a bright girl, though, and when a man takes her to a bar she suppresses her impulses and orders what he does or else says "Scotch on the rocks." (The only innate fault in women as drinkers is that they think too highly of Scotch.) All her friends are civilized and so she has always had decent cocktails in the home. The trouble comes when she decides to wipe the slate clean and have twenty people in to cocktails. Her boss would have been fired long since if she didn't do his thinking for him. She can show the Income Tax people exactly where they are misconstruing their own regulations. She can beat the racket at a fur sale. But the moment she starts thinking about giving a cocktail party in her own apartment her self-confidence begins to ooze away. The insecurity of the single gnaws at her and by the time she has made out the list of guests, she's licked. She makes straight for a cookbook.

Nothing is going to change that. She will always make for a cookbook till one of those parties achieves its purpose—we know that nineteen of the twenty guests are just smokescreen—and he proves it to her in their own pantry. The only thing to do is to change the cookbook.

And a good idea from every point of view. So, not only for a million women and twenty million stomachs they would not knowingly endanger but also on behalf of public enlightenment, I offer the following without fee or royalty to all publishers who will contract to substitute it for the Beverage section in their handbooks.

The Enemy

Ce qu'il faut connaître des coktels
Pour les hôstesses

1. Relax, sister; it's easy. And the more you'll relax, the easier it will be. Memorize this: simplicity, integrity, nothing mysterious, nothing fancy, nothing sweet.

2. Throw away that bottle of grenadine. Never buy another one.

3. Leave today's special at the liquor store alone: it's for cause. The reason the man cut the price on that stuff is that he couldn't move it; people recognized it as what it is. Go without lunch for a couple of weeks if you have to, or cut the guests from twenty to ten. Cheap liquor is grudge liquor.

4. Get two whiskeys, Scotch and either rye or bourbon. (I'm being easy on your budget. A rye

man won't be offended by bourbon or vice versa but Scotch drinkers want Scotch and you've got to give it to them. Never touch the stuff myself.) Bonded rye or bourbon; or, if you really are hard up, unbonded but straight. Never a blend, even a blend of straight whiskeys. Some charged water; perfectly sound people may want a highball at the cocktail hour—they're going to stop off at a couple of other parties before dinner. No ginger ale—I said, no ginger ale. A bottle of the driest sherry; ask a friend you trust what brand he likes. (Cool it a little if you want to but don't chill it—you might as well boil it. Don't have much to do with people who drink sherry at any time except with the soup; there's something wrong with them. It's inoffensive, though, so long as it's dry.) Get American gin and get it in the highest price range. Cheap gin is for hangovers; whatever imported gin may be for, it isn't for martinis.

84

5. Orange bitters make a good astringent for the face. Never put them in anything that is to be drunk.

6. Nothing sweet. If I'm repeating myself it's because I know you and have got to check up on you.

7. Remember what I've said about ice. Your neighborhood store sells it. About a dollar's worth.

8. Turn down the thermostat.

9. If somebody insists on an old-fashioned and you see no way out, dissolve the damn sugar in a little water before you put the whiskey in—it won't dissolve in alcohol. If somebody asks for one made of Scotch, say no, politely if you can manage to, but say no.

10. Nothing sweet, and that goes double for vermouth.

11. I have already declared the gospel in full but let's make the main points again. Martinis, slugs of whiskey, highballs, and if you must an old-fashioned. Nothing else. You don't care to know anybody who wants anything else. And everything you serve must be cold. No surplus, no dividend, nothing for the pot. Mix every round from scratch.

12. Let's be clear about this: no Manhattans and no rum.

As I have shown, my dear (see how a properly made drink softens a man), it's easy to make a good martini and it is impossible not to make a good slug of whiskey if you've got good whiskey and a confiding nature. But for God's sake, develop a little skill and then do the job unostentatiously. We don't drink cocktails on our knees and there's no point in making them that way; so no ritual, be offhand, be casual and decently fast. An appearance of habituated ease will get you off to a running start with that guy. He will equate sound liquor with sound gal and the second round will do things to your figure that Elizabeth Arden could not do for you in three months. You're in, darling, and all you had to do was steer clear of chartreuse, egg white, and cyanide.

Subsidiary matters are not within my province but so many of you phone in about a couple of them that I might as well tell you where the rules committee stands. Actually, if you'll supply a couple of good cheeses and a couple of kinds of good crackers, you won't have to serve anything else. Make one of them ordinary American cheddar, as snappy as it comes, and the other a fairly high one. In any event, don't serve anything fussy and the woman who mixes cream cheese and Roquefort and stuffs celery with it does not belong among us.

And there is no hangover in our liquor unless you are too young for your own good. Get the kind of liquor I've told you to and use it properly and you'll face the dawn without a flutter or a qualm and so will all your guests. But maybe one of them takes more than we have learned is bright? Or maybe that guy doesn't respond as fast as you had hoped and you take one or two above yourself? Well, a vast deal of nonsense is talked about preventives and cures of hangovers. Practically all of it is talked by people we don't want in the house. Only the Chuck and Mable type I'll be telling you about in a minute would swallow cream or olive oil or such stuff beforehand—what a hell of a way to approach a good hour and a good drink! Or that folklore about Vitamin B. If I must speak plainly, anyone who takes a massive dose of Vitamin B will within an hour need to bathe with Lifebuoy or stay out in the open air. If I must continue to speak plainly, don't overdrink.

But since you ask me, here's what your family doctor does when he finds that the last two have crept upon him unaware. It's a three-shot treatment, best taken before going to bed but also effective tomorrow morning. Up to a teaspoonful of baking soda in a glass of water, or the equivalent of some other alkalizer. Twenty grains of aspirin or some other mild opiate. And three-quarters of a grain to a grain and a half (depending on how you react to it) of nembutal, seconal, or any other barbiturate of equal strength. Stomach, head, jitters — that does it. And next time pull up at the three-quarters post.

I've been talking about people who go wrong through ignorance or unfortunate upbringing, not wickedness, and about portions of American culture where the blight is curable. Now for the corruption that has honeycombed enormous sections of a fair and pleasant land, and for the enemy, the barbarians, the real bastards. It is alarmingly probable that you don't know how fearful this decadence is or how widely it has spread. We are amiable people, our kindly sentiments kept active by the kindly liquor we drink, and disposed to believe that in a country of equal opportunity for all, the natural goodness of mankind will lead everyone to cultivate the same excellence we practice. That is a dangerous state of mind; it could open the city and the citadel to the screeching horde while we talked at ease over a martini. Which is why I had better, in all humility, tell you my own experience; it brought me to grips with evil and its harsh moral is that the underground can get to members of a man's own family.

It befell at Christmas time, a season when we think charitably of nearly everyone and everything. Chimes in church steeples fill the lavender evening with carols almost as heartwarming as the sound of martinis stirred in a pitcher, and after a couple that have been stirred properly the carols from loudspeakers along the avenue are not really offensive. We glow with loving-kindness and the fellowship is willing to relax its discipline and let those of its members who have a strong sense of

Hot drinks

are for people who have

had skiing accidents,

though it is an open question

whether anyone who skis

is worth giving liquor to

or his life worth saving.

ceremony drink eggnog or Tom and Jerry. . . . Not me. Not, I judge, any of the purest. Hot drinks are for people who have had skiing accidents, though it is an open question whether anyone who skis is worth giving liquor to or his life worth saving. Cream and eggs have their place but that place is not an alcoholic drink, and it is no more right to foul up honest liquor with them than to poison it with spinach juice. You give them to invalids? I don't know why. True, every invalid, every sufferer, everyone to whom your sympathy goes out, will be cheered, strengthened, and restored by a slug of good whiskey. Or half a dozen, decently spaced. But don't confuse whiskey with diet and don't mix them. Remember always that the three abominations are: (1) rum, (2) any other sweet drink, and (3) any mixed drink except one made of gin and dry vermouth in the ratio I have given.

What's that? Does this hold for punches? See here, have I got to stick my neck out about everything? Well, you asked for a ruling. It is true that many stirring scenes and high moments in the American past are associated with punch. But our national past contained other things we would not countenance now and can't be proud of. So does our personal past. I confess that there were times when I drank punch, even times when I persuaded myself it wasn't as awful as it tasted. When I was young I was as foolish as the next one, and I went through the whole repertoire, both ways from Fish House, including the traditional punches of elegant and select societies and the even more fearful ones that have come down in some very odd family lines. Let's be honest. There is no such thing as a good punch; there isn't even a drinkable one. It's sweet, isn't it? It's mixed, isn't it? It has got rum in it, hasn't it? It is invariably an ignoble thing, it is made to serve liquor to people economically—if you can't serve good liquor to a lot of people, serve good liquor to a few people. Put it this way. Maybe you

94

like a good Burgundy, or a Pouilly, or a Champagne. How would you like it mixed with root beer and Veg-8?

As I was saying. There had been premonitory signs, like the froth that runs in a stream ahead of a flood, but I did not recognize them for what they were. I saw listed among the *New Yorker*'s suggestions for Christmas gifts an expensive machine which at a touch of one button would deliver three gin and at touch of another button one of vermouth. I tolerantly reflected that among my friends are some who, if they received this obscenity for Christmas, would need a new gin button long before the vermouth one showed wear, and then fatuously forgot about it. Next, walking up Fifth Avenue, I stopped to look at a jeweler's window and saw there a satin-lined case somewhat larger than a woman's traveling bag, containing a corkscrew, a bottle opener, and a silver jigger, all with large, ornate horn handles and the set priced

at $85. (Probably $150 this year and on sale at a thousand places.) With the same foolish tolerance I thought, ah, yes, the rich—and though this was a pustule of the plague before my eyes, thought no more. But my heedlessness was shattered on Christmas morning. I found at the foot of the tree—no flinching now, let's face it, they were given to me by my wife—a dozen glass stirring-rods, each containing a thermometer and each thermometer marked with a green-colored zone between 50° and 32°, the zone, said the box top, of proper and pleasurable drinking. This horrified me and I was aroused at last but panic did not strike till a few days later, when the mail brought me a catalogue from a shop where I had once bought a cocktail shaker: a simple, undecorated article, I take my oath, a clear glass pitcher of convenient size, with a handle and a lip that facilitates pouring—in no way quaint or cute. That catalogue spread the full horror before me and I saw what evil had spread

among my countrymen while I drowsed in lotos
land, an honest drink in a plain glass in my hand. I
sought out other catalogues. I visited many stores
and made many inquiries. There had been no error or mistake; the evidence of the first catalogue
stands. Fashionable household-goods shops sell the
same cloacal objects, gifte shoppes sell them, your
favorite department store sells them, the terrifying
truth is that you cannot walk half a mile in any business district in the United States without finding
some of them offered for sale—and sold.

What is it like in a house where the family has
been seized by some fearful madness such as the tar-
antelle? What is it like when you visit such a house
and find strangers once your friends staring at you
with bright eyes out of delusions that report to them
images of fever, hallucinatory images of nothing that
exists in the clean, sane world? I can give you an idea,
for I can tell you what it is like in the American home
that has made drinking whimsical.

Chuck, the host, is wearing a white canvas apron that has stamped on it a picture of a mustached bartender shaking up a drink; droll legends have been painted on the bar and block capitals above the bartender's head read, "Name your Pizen, Gents." Chuck's wife Mable has on a similar apron that makes her appear to be clad in a big corset with exaggerated falsie-cups and ever so funny umbrella drawers, you know, gay-nineties stuff, daring as all hell. If the kiddies have not yet been sent upstairs with a handful of marshmallows from Chuck's bar, they are dancing up and down and screaming with laughter, costumed in little aprons just like Popsie's and Mom's. Signs have been tacked up in the hall: a pointing hand which says "To the Bar. Check your Morals," or "Don't Take Yourself So Blamed Seriously," or "Danger: Men Drinking," or up to a dozen others just as witty. Mable likes to protect her furniture—and God knows she has to, with the people she entertains—but in the spirit of things likes to

Let's be honest.
There is no such thing
as a good punch;
there isn't even a
drinkable one.

do so with hospitable glee. So she has set up "Cutie
Coastrays," each of which has "a different gay gag"
(such as "Danger: Hangover Under Construction"),
or perhaps the set of eight will show a stripteaser in
successive stages of her act.

All this sets a gay mood and wins jolly smiles
from the guests but the really hilarious merriment
does not begin till Chuck gets to work. He has a
"torso squeezer" for limes, though the designation
is inaccurate for it isn't in the shape of a torso, it's
a pair of legs, daringly naked. (He also has a bottle
stopper with legs issuing from it.) There are torsos
on some muddlers but they will be discovered only
by discerning people who hold one to the light so
that it casts the shadow of a breast. He has bottle
stoppers with torsos on them too, some bound with
what you can be sure he calls a "bras" but some, hot
damn!, quite nude. He has lots of bottle openers,
all comical but discarded as he found funnier gags.
He is not likely to surpass the newest one, which

101

he now leads off with. It is called Horse's Rosette and the catalogue says, "it's the 'south end' of a Chestnut horse done in natural rich russet." Chuck backs it over a bottle cap and the roar of laughter he gets is worth the four-fifty he paid for it.

That is only the first roar. When you take a cigarette the box plays "How Dry I Am." One of Chuck's bottles plays the same tune, another one "For He's a Jolly Good Fellow," and if you go upstairs "one of the world's greatest laugh producers" will play one, loudly, on the toilet-paper roll. Want a cocktail? (Chuck calls them that.) He uses a shaker waggishly made in the form of a dinner bell, with a handle to swing it by. That's for tonight—he has another one that looks like a fire extinguisher though it's stamped "Thirst Extinguisher" of course, and a third that has very stewed roisterers on it and a fourth with formulas for half a dozen reliable vomitories. Your cocktail glass narrows to a rounded base so that you cannot set it down—we don't linger over drinks here—and a female nude is stretched over that bottom. (Bottom, see: convulsing.) Or maybe tonight the glasses with tipsy stems remind you it's brave and manly to get soused, or, more likely, Chuck uses those whose stems are nude women which, the page says, will make the guest more interested in the glass than in the drink. If you don't want a cocktail—and you don't—the highball glass will have comic souses on it, maybe, or an electric bulb in the base will light up when you take it off the table.

Maybe; but in his glassware (and every other adjunct of the bar where it's possible) Chuck prefers to bring whimsy and liquor and nudity together. He has retired the glasses that had prankish pink elephants on them and all the others that were just gags, however sidesplitting. The new ones are all girls. The girls are wearing clothes on the outside of the glass, the side someone else sees, but as you drink you make out that, on the inside, either they

103

Orange bitters
make a good astringent
for the face.
Never put them
in anything that is to
be drunk.

are taking off their clothes or they didn't have any on to begin with. Another set has girls who are dressed when you pour the drink in but naked after the picture has soaked for a while. But the one Chuck thinks is the drollest has an opaque frosting except that a clear space has been left in the shape of a keyhole, and as you drink, oh, boy, what you can see through that keyhole!

Lots of other naked and half-dressed girls too. The legs on the bottle stopper. The bottle stopper with the other half of a naked girl on it, the one with half a girl in a bras, and another one with a girl in bras and panties, for you can be quite sure Chuck calls them panties. And don't miss the set of eight mugs whose handles are nudes successively sprawling toward the rim and finally falling over it. Next to undressed girls the funniest gags are souses. Some of the glasses have souses on them, some have wisecracks about getting soused, there are drunks on lampshades and trays, game-room walls are spotted

with framed jokes about hangovers and falling upstairs. And one of Chuck's "pourers"—a pourer is a
gadget you put over the neck of the bottle—is in the
shape of a drunk hanging on to a lamppost. He has
a red nose, for humor, and he's holding out a bottle
which is the spout you pour through; the lamp on
the post lights up and it's marked "Say When."

Chuck certainly has done it up brown. There
are lots of other gags, some of them neither girly
nor stewed, just laughable. There are stoppers that
look like hillbillies, Mexicans, Frenchies, Indians,
hobos. Some of the pourers shut themselves off
and some make cracks about Scotch—means stin-
gy. Funniest damn thing he's got, though, is the hat
he presently offers you or puts on himself; it has
an ice bag in the crown and a bandage for the fore-
head and ear plugs and pockets for Bromo Seltzer,
and the wisecracks printed on it would double you
up. He has bottles that look like everything except
bottles and a bar radio that looks like a bottle. He

has six-in-one implements that will do anything to a drink except swallow it, big hammers for little ice cubes, a tray that looks like a violin, paper napkins with limericks on them, ash trays in the shape of false teeth, comical dolls that hold pretzels and potato chips, and everywhere you turn big cards with formulas for drinks.

You know what the formulas are. They're just like the ones in the cookbooks, only they're witty and have wicked allusions to girls scattered through them. They tell you to mix milk and honey with Scotch. Or crème de cassis and sweet vermouth and rye and soda. Or pour some whiskey over tansy leaves. Or Irish and grenadine. Or sloe gin and dry vermouth and Scotch and bitters and phosphate and powdered sugar and a little nutmeg on top. Or stir into whatever liquor you're using some whipped cream laced with grenadine. Or to bourbon add grenadine mixed with strong Pekoe and curaçao and evaporated milk and confectioner's sugar and

The martini is a city
dweller, a metropolitan.
It is not to be drunk
beside a mountain stream
or anywhere else
in the wilds...

———✦✦✦———

cinnamon. Merely to read them threatens to produce emesis and there is greater nausea in realizing
that these things are actually drunk. They are drunk
by Chuck in a funny hat and Mable who has just
wound up the music box in the toilet and their group
of merry friends, from glasses which light up and dis-
play a blonde taking off her skirt.

My country, oh, my country! these are the louts
who but for the fellowship could bring thee down.
But, brethren, give them one moment of compas-
sion—so little aware of liquor, so little worthy of
it, that they must make it coy and cute and leer-
ing, of such small personal resources that it can free
them to no wellbeing of their own. They do not like
the goodness of good liquor, for they kill its taste
with disgusting things. They do not get from it the
reconciliation that knits up the raveled day for you
and me, for they have to buy their wit on printed
cards. They have not got the imagination nor the
companionableness nor the human sensitiveness

that good drinking nurtures to a glow. They drink their messes to the end that a slight mechanical lewdness may seem daring. That they may look at a woman and a drink of liquor without panic. That they may bray with a brassy laughter when some-one fresh from a jokeshop produces still another glass, this time in the shape of a chamberpot. Even the stimulation they get is not the benevolence of alcohol but systemic poisoning, a rebellion of the stomach against the filth they pour into it. To their infantile minds there is something glorious and heroic in getting drunk and yet for all their daring they never get there. It is not drunkenness that makes them pass out on a game-room floor littered with last century's vaudeville jokes, not drunkenness, just botulism.

One moment only, then put pity away from you. For if they live, the city and our fellowship will fall. Sound the trumpet and set up our standard in the square. From all parts of the city the honest, the virtuous, and the kindly will repair to it. To the sewer with their drinks, smash their glassware in the fireplace, and that mug whose handle is a bent and gartered knee will make a useful bludgeon for their skulls. Death and damnation to Chuck, Mable, and all their progeny and friends, to the last of them without heir or issue, till the air is pure again and we can walk the streets of a clean and quiet city, aware that we have saved our heritage.

And speedily. For it's getting on toward six o'clock.

4

⁓⧉⁓

The Hour

THE VISION IS FOR THE APPOINTED TIME.
It would be good to know what great man discovered distillation. We never will, but when
his earliest disciples were finding out what a still
could do words too had power. The water of life,
they called the mystery, *aqua vitae, eau de vie*. They
spoke well.

May six o'clock never find you alone. The mystery's heart of hearts is mutuality. Men put down their packs to share the vanishing-away, nor can a man hold a weapon in one hand if he has a drink in the other. But if you should be alone when evening comes on, then this benignant spirit is a good companion. Not by first choice a bar unless you are benighted on the road or in the streets, but if so then surely a bar—and worth going a fur piece, or a right smart one, to find the proper kind. Better perhaps a club. Avoid the University Club, any college club, for it will be full of young men. The young are not unsound as such—it is they who, properly schooled, must succeed us. But it does take them an unconscionable time to learn that we do not hold football rallies at six o'clock. Throughout the last quartering of the sun it has been an open question if we would make it and the odds grew longer with the shadows. We have crossed the line with spectral fingers missing us by only a hairsbreadth.

In the moment when we realize that we have made it after all and the heart whispers Not Today, we want no noise. A loud voice afflicts the ear worse than drums, though raised in comradeship, and song is not to be borne.

Much can be said for the kind of club called stuffy. For one thing, the bartender must meet the constant criticism of experienced and discriminating men, the best of whom also compose the Cellar Committee and buy thoughtfully. For another, propriety and age combine to make the membership speak in whispers. For fifteen years I have belonged to such a club and though that term has brought me to the estate where my friends' grandchildren stand up and offer me their chairs, I still remain a probationer plugging for the first form. If I hear a whisper speaking of "the war" I know it is not my war, which was also Black Jack Pershing's, but at the latest Admiral Dewey's and more likely the one our Confederate members won.

This is an hour of
diminishing,
of slowing down,
of quieting.

So it is a good place to reach just ahead of the pursuing feet. Tiptoeing across the almost dark cavern of the lounge (at the hour all lamps should be shaded and only a few of them lit, for if the body is in shadow the soul will the sooner turn toward the sun), I take my drink to a chair so big that one's head cannot be seen above its back, by a window that faces a cross-town street. We are near enough the avenue to hear the traffic diminishing. This is an hour of diminishing, of slowing down, of quieting. Thus islanded in dimness and the murmur of traffic fading toward silence, one is apt for the ministration. Calm against background tumult is an essential of the hour; it is the firelight shining through the cabin window on the snow of the forest, the strong shack beside a lake whose waters a gale is hurling up the shore.

(Cabin. The martini is a city dweller, a metropolitan. It is not to be drunk beside a mountain stream or anywhere else in the wilds, not in the open there

or even indoors. And this is not due to the facts that one must carry two kinds of liquor and that ice is hard to come by. I have sometimes taken gin and vermouth with me to the wilderness my trade requires me to visit and by good staff work have located ice. A martini is never bad and I could not be brought to dispraise it but it does not harmonize with campfires and sleeping bags. It does not feel at home on river boats, either—on any small boats. Whiskey is forthright and therefore better here. All cultural subtleties belong to the city—where else are women beautiful?)

Which brings us to Marjorie. At six o'clock take Marjorie to a bar. And now we must be certain it is the right bar. This is one of the most satisfying of all the settings and combinations that life affords. And we owe it—we owe both Marjorie and the bar—to the age which I have said was mostly dark, to Prohibition. Prohibition sanctioned women to share liquor with men frankly, without

surreptitiousness or shame. For the unilateral saloon—a pier and anchorage and buttress of virtuous living but sometimes of unpleasing decor and
often much too boisterous at six o'clock—it sub-
stituted the speakeasy. The speakeasy was quietly
decorated and happily illuminated, and both the
pretense of secrecy and the presence of women
enforced quiet behavior and good manners. When
Repeal came we had the sense to apply the lesson
and a good bar today is indistinguishable from a
good speakeasy of 1930.

Quiet and softly lighted, of course, not neces-
sarily tiny but at least small, only a few stools for
the solitary, and if banquettes then not violently
colored, if booths then not cramped. There is no
more fitting place for the slackening of exigency,
the withdrawal of necessity. Time is extensible, no
hour must be met, there is no pressure to go anywhere else—we could eat next door but we'll take
that up later on, don't bother about it now. She is

a pretty woman and she will be prettier very soon.
And she cannot sustain now the contrarieties of
other hours and moods; they yield to the sovereign
solvent. So it is Marjorie's presence that reveals the
fullest meaning of the water of life; what it truly
dissolves away is loneliness. She and good liquor at
6:00 P.M.—two warmths, two tendernesses, have
met in the martini of the heart.

Better still in Marjorie's own place, which
should be several stories higher than my club window so that the slowing traffic may be still softer
and the evening colors more fully seen, or in your
own if by good fortune you have married her. There
should always be a woman at the hour, to make the
renewal richer, to augment the beauties of evening
and ease and alcohol, to orchestrate life's appetites.
But though this may easily be love's hour it is not
passion's, and though Marjorie is an enhancement,
the fullness of fellowship extends beyond two,
though not far beyond. The mystery, I have said, is

How fastidiously cold
a second martini is to the palate
but how warm to the heart,
being drunk.
What you seem to hear
is not distant music
but hope re-echoing in a
now-lighted secrecy.

magnanimous, expansive, social: it sinks the ego in benediction.

A woman I know who makes so good a martini that she must be seeded with the ranking ten is usually forced to put her art to a use that will illustrate what I mean. She is married to a lawyer and he is a good man, but he will never pass the screening that admits to the last circle. Late afternoon finds him, as it finds you and me, with all lost but courage, fighting honor's rear-guard action without hope. The penumbra grows and you know as well as I do what snarling the wind carries. My friend slips out of humanity, even as we do, and when with detached amazement he sees that he has lasted till the end of the day's job, like us he starts homeward fully aware that he has no chance of making it. That last shuddering half-hour!—the soul shredded to excelsior, the heart deaf and blind, the nerves carrying the overload that will burn out the last fuse. Like us he hears the jaws snap shut behind him as he goes through the door. But mark what happens now. He makes for a hot bath. And there he lies steaming and his accomplished wife serves him martinis that have the halo of perfection.

No. This is too little spiritual; there is too much selfishness, too much ego, too much disregard. It forfeits too much. Bad enough to reduce a free spirit and an artist to a servitor, but worse to monopolize artist and art, focus the hour on himself, and scorn the fellowship.

Build the citadel strong. I give you instead the knowledge that when you open that door on liberation there will be not only Marjorie but two or three or even four friends too. If one or two are women, let them be like Marjorie, soft-spoken, rewarding to look at, of quick intuition. Let the children play quietly apart or be locked in the coal cellar. The room quiet, the lamps shaded, dusk beyond the windows, and on the little table a big bowl of ice, and more vermouth and gin than we can possibly want. Whiskey if you say so, but why?—Marjorie and I have mastered the martini.

The moment of tableau is far finer than that when the house lights go out, the footlights go on, and the conductor raises his baton to bring the strings and woodwinds in on the first beat. He has no symphony so rich as ours. Does it matter what the newsboys are yelling in the street? There. With that taste illusion ebbs away; the water of life has swept us into its current.

The rat stops gnawing in the wood, the dungeon walls withdraw, the weight is lifted. Nerve ends that stuck through your skin like bristles when you blotted the last line or shut the office door behind you have withdrawn into their sheaths. Your pulse steadies and the sun has found your heart. You were wrong about the day, you did more admirably than you believed, you did well enough, you did well. The day was not bad, the season has not been bad, there is sense and even promise in going on.

How fastidiously cold a second martini is to the palate but how warm to the heart, being drunk. What you seem to hear is not distant music but hope re-echoing in a now-lighted secrecy. These are good men, wise, considerate, indomitable. There is more richness than you remembered and you your-self have rediscovered the wit and sureness that the illusion hid. Observe the pinkness in Marjorie's cheeks, the eagerness in her eyes; she is shrewdly and subtly formed; how sagacious the way she has done her hair, how pleasant her dress, how respon-sive her fingers.

The walls are breached. Are down. There were no walls.

Certainly I'll have another one. The water of life was given to us to make us see for a while that we are more nearly men and women, more nearly kind and gentle and generous, pleasanter and stronger, than without its vision there is any evidence we are. It is the healer, the weaver of forgiveness and reconciliation, the justifier of us to ourselves and one another. One more, and then with a spirit made whole again in a cleansed world, to dinner.

May six o'clock never
find you alone.
The mystery's heart of
hearts is mutuality.